FIRST
PEOPLES
of NORTH
AMERICA

THE PEOPLE AND CULTURE OF THE
CHUMASH

JOEL NEWSOME
RAYMOND BIAL

Cavendish
Square
New York

Published in 2017 by Cavendish Square Publishing, LLC
243 5th Avenue, Suite 136, New York, NY 10016

Library of Congress Cataloging-in-Publication Data

Names: Newsome, Joel, 1984- author. | Bial, Raymond, author.
Title: The people and culture of the Chumash / Joel Newsome and Raymond Bial.
Description: New York : Cavendish Square Publishing, [2017] | Series: First peoples of North America | Includes bibliographical references and index.
Identifiers: LCCN 2016035597 (print) | LCCN 2016035977 (ebook) |
ISBN 9781502622556 (library bound) | ISBN 9781502622563 (E-book)
Subjects: LCSH: Chumash Indians--History--Juvenile literature. | Chumash Indians--Social life and customs--Juvenile literature.
Classification: LCC E99.C815 B53 2017 (print) | LCC E99.C815 (ebook) |
DDC 979.4004/9758--dc23
LC record available at https://lccn.loc.gov/2016035597

Editorial Director: David McNamara
Editor: Kristen Susienka
Copy Editor: Rebecca Rohan
Associate Art Director: Amy Greenan
Production Coordinator: Karol Szymczuk
Photo Research: J8 Media

The photographs in this book are used by permission and through the courtesy of: Cover Bobbi Onia/Underwood Archives/Getty Images; p. 6 Eyal Nahmias/Alamy Stock Photo; p. 8 Wikimedia Commons/TastyCakes/File:Santa Cruz Island.jpg/CC BY 3.0; p. 10 Planet Observer/UIG/Bridgeman Images; pp. 12-13 Marc Solomon/StockByte/ Getty Images; pp. 16-17, 18, 22, 46-47, 48-49, 50, 54, 58, 64, Raymond Bial; pp. 24-35 TFoxFoto/Shutterstock.com; pp. 26-27 Underwood Archives/UIG/Bridgeman Images; pp. 30-31 Debra Behr/Alamy Stock Photo; pp. 32-33 Nativestock.com; p. 35 Joel P. Lugavere/Los Angeles Times/Getty Images; p. 38 Chuck Place/Alamy Stock Photo; p. 45 javi02/iStock/Thinkstock.com; p. 60 Nik Wheeler/Corbis Documentary/Getty Images; p. 68 Gary Ombler/ Dorling Kindersley/Getty Images; p. 71 Ken Lee Photography; p. 72-73 Lisa Werner/Moment/Getty Images; p. 77 Nativestock Pictures/Bridgeman Images; p. 78 Bryan Chan/Los Angeles Times via Getty Images; p. 82 Underwood Archives/Getty Images; p. 85 Wikimedia Commons/File:Vizcaino.jpg/Public Domain; p. 86 Wikimedia Commons/ File:Santa Barbara Mission, Cal. (pcard-print-pub-pc-16a).jpg/Public Domain; p. 89 Wikimedia Commons/ Harrington papers, National Anthropical Archives, Smithsonian Institution /File:Chmash musicians 1873.jpg/ Public Domain; p. 96 William Langdon/National Geographic Creative/Bridgeman Images; p. 99 Rainer Lesniewski/ Shutterstock.com; p. 100 Boris Yaro/Los Angeles Times/Getty Images; pp. 102-103 Michael Robinson Chavez/Los Angeles Times/Getty Images; pp. 104-105 Anacleto Rapping/Los Angeles Times/Getty Images; p. 106, Black Gold Cooperative Library System; p. 108 National Anthropical Archives, Smithsonian Institution.

Printed in the United States of America

ACKNOWLEDGMENTS

This book would not have been possible without the generous help of many individuals and organizations that have dedicated themselves to honoring the customs of the Chumash.

We would like to thank in particular Cavendish Square Publishing and all who contributed to finding photos and other materials for publication. Finally, we would like to thank our families and friends for their encouragement and support along our writing journey.

CONTENTS

A Chumash girl wears brightly colored traditional clothing and jewelry.

AUTHORS' NOTE

At the dawn of the twentieth century, Native Americans were thought to be a vanishing race. However, despite four hundred years of warfare, deprivation, and disease, Native Americans have not gone away. Countless thousands have lost their lives, but over the course of the twentieth century, the populations of Native tribes have grown tremendously. Even as Native Americans struggle to adapt to modern Western life, they have also kept the flame of their traditions alive—the language, religion, stories, and the everyday ways of life. An exhilarating renaissance in Native American culture is now sweeping the nation from coast to coast.

The First Peoples of North America books depict the social and cultural life of the major nations, from the early history of native peoples in North America to their present-day struggles for survival and dignity. Historical and contemporary photographs of traditional subjects, as well as period illustrations, are blended throughout each book so that readers may gain a sense of family life in a tipi, a hogan, a longhouse, or in houses today.

No single book can comprehensively portray the intricate and varied lifeways of an entire tribe, or nation. We only hope that young people will come away with a deeper appreciation for the rich tapestry of Native culture—both then and now—and a keen desire to learn more about these first Americans.

Many of the first Chumash settled near the coasts of California.

CHAPTER ONE

What was passed is what we are today.

—Ernestine De Soto, Chumash elder

A CULTURE BEGINS

Native Americans have lived in North America for thousands of years. One group called the Chumash came to live in what is now southwestern California. We cannot be certain when the ancestors of the Chumash first inhabited these areas, but archaeologists estimate they arrived between twelve thousand and twenty-seven thousand years ago. They had a network of villages that encompassed vast areas

California was the Chumash's home. Over the centuries, the land they lived on changed. Many Chumash eventually lived in missions started by the Spanish.

The People and Culture of the Chumash

of modern-day Los Angeles, Santa Barbara, and San Luis Obispo Counties. They also lived on the nearby islands of Santa Cruz, San Miguel, Santa Rosa, and Anacapa. As generations passed, the Chumash developed their societies and eventually endured massive difficulties with the arrival of Spanish **missionaries**, forever changing their culture and communities.

Origins of a People

The Chumash were not a single tribe or nation. They formed a loosely allied network of seventy-five to one hundred independent villages in southern and central California. The people in these communities spoke six to eight distinct, yet related, languages. Before the arrival of the Spanish, the Chumash territory encompassed about 7,000 square miles (18,123 square kilometers), with villages located in three regions: the Channel Islands, the Pacific Coast, and the interior mountains. The Island Chumash lived on Santa Cruz, Santa Rosa, San Miguel, and Anacapa Islands of the Channel Islands. The Coastal Chumash, which included the Ventureño, Barbareño, Ynezeño, Purisimeño, and the Obispeño, lived along the coast. The Interior Chumash lived in the mountains. The name "Chumash," now used for all these groups, was originally a Coastal Chumash word that referred only to the Island Chumash living on Santa Rosa Island. The similar name "Michumash" referred to the people of Santa Cruz Island.

Most of the villages were clustered along 250 miles (402 kilometers) of the Pacific Coast, from San Luis Obispo to Malibu Canyon. The coastal communities

were usually situated along the mouths of streams and
rivers, which supplied fresh water and a means of travel
by canoe. The villages of the Interior Chumash were
tucked away among the jagged mountains of present-
day Santa Barbara County. They lived as far as 75 miles
(121 km) inland, to the western edge of the San
Joaquin Valley. The spiritual heart of Chumash territory
was Mount Pinos, which towers to nearly 9,000 feet
(2,743 meters) and is northeast of Santa Barbara.

Mount Pinos, seen in the distance at the end of the road, was central to Chumash beliefs.

Tracing their ancestry from an ancient people known as Milling Stone Indians, the Chumash have lived in this region for more than ten thousand years. Over many generations, they developed one of Native California's most complex societies. By the sixteenth century, the scattered villages shared a similar political and social organization and customs. They had also established an extensive trade network. Before the arrival of the Spanish, the population of the Chumash may have been as few as eight thousand or as many as twenty-two thousand.

From one generation to the next, the Chumash relied on the land and water to provide them with food, clothing, and shelter. However, from the moment of first contact with Europeans in the sixteenth century, the Chumash way of life began to change dramatically.

A Changing Landscape

During the Ice Age, when glaciers stored much of the earth's water, the oceans were lower. The Channel Islands were joined to the mainland by a peninsula that extended from the Santa Barbara mainland. Many animals, including mammoths, moved westward onto the peninsula and became isolated when the glaciers melted and the rising ocean again separated the islands from the mainland. As the sea levels remained stable, unique animals evolved on the islands, including a dwarf mammoth (now extinct) and distinct species of fox, skunk, and mice. Unusual plants, such as a rare kind of ironwood, also developed on the islands. The climate was mild for most of the year. However, strong winds, often carrying a veil of misty rain, occasionally swept over the islands, especially during the winter.

The geography of each island was distinct. San Miguel, the westernmost island, was marked by ridges of sandstone and volcanic rock. Two hills rose from the middle of the island, much of which was once blanketed with sumac and manzanita, along with shifting dunes. There were no streams on this island— just one spring near Cuyler Harbor and a few seeps of freshwater in the rocks. East of San Miguel lies the larger island of Santa Rosa. Its rounded hills were carpeted with grass, bushes, and cactus. Canyons held freshwater springs and streams, as well as clusters of oak and pine trees. On its small, eastern coast, there were stretches of beach and ranges of low cliffs. East of Santa Rosa was the island of Santa Cruz. The largest of the four islands, Santa Cruz, consisted of towering mountains from the ocean, the tallest of which reached to 2,400 feet (731 m). Stands of oak, pine, and island ironwood thrived in the one large valley. There were also deep ravines laced by streams of clear water. The coastline was composed of many high, formidable cliffs, but the island also had a few beaches of cobblestones on which the Chumash were able to land their canoes. Located east of Santa Cruz and just 12 miles (19 km) from the mainland, Anacapa was the smallest of the islands. It was actually a group of three small islands, all made up of volcanic rock. The Anacapas are in the form of flat-topped plateaus and range from 90 to 300 feet (27 to 91 m) high. Most of the island was bounded by sheer cliffs, but the Chumash gathered abalone from among the shallow rocks on the north shore. They also hunted seals and sea lions that occupied areas of the island. Because there was little fresh water on the island, the Chumash visited Anacapa only seasonally, establishing fishing camps there.

Most of the Chumash lived along the coast of the mainland directly across the **channel** from the islands. Here, the waves of the Pacific Ocean lapped the sandy, rock-strewn beaches of a narrow coastal plain. Just beyond the glimmering shoreline, cliffs rose suddenly, like rocky shelves. The cliffs not only offered a

The People and Culture of the Chumash

The Chumash built their homes and communities within California's landscape.

Some Chumash lived farther inland, near California's mountains and streams.

The People and Culture of the Chumash

breathtaking view of the Pacific Ocean but also hinted at the difficult terrain farther inland. Just beyond the cliffs rose that portion of the southern Coast Ranges known as the Santa Ynez Mountains. Covered with **chaparral** and dense forests, these mountains reached high into the cloud–dappled sky. Along the coastal plain, the climate remained mild throughout the year, and the ocean provided a rich bounty of food. Many Chumash settled here in villages strung along the coast from Ventura to Point Conception. Other groups of Coastal Chumash settled as far north as Estero Bay. Here, the smooth beaches rose to sandy dunes, and then abruptly to rocky terraces and hills, occasionally interrupted by small valleys and streams. Still other coastal groups had their villages east of Ventura and south to Malibu Canyon. Closely related to these coastal dwellers were nearby island groups that had villages along the Santa Ynez and Santa Clara Rivers.

The Interior Chumash lived among the mountains and rivers between the San Joaquin Valley and the Santa Ynez River. They were divided into three groups: the Cuyama, the Emigdiano, and the Castac. Their varied territory included a barren stretch called the Carrizo Plain, lush grasslands dotted with oak trees, and mountains blanketed with thick forests. Here, the Chumash had to deal with very hot summers and chilly winters, yet they had a bounty of food from plants and animals. In the craggy land of peaks and valleys, the Interior Chumash left hundreds of startlingly beautiful and mysterious rock paintings hidden away in caves.

Chumash Belief and Storytelling

For thousands of years, the Chumash lived in scattered villages along the Pacific Coast, on the Channel Islands, and in the mountains of the Coast Ranges of southern California. They hunted, fished, and gathered to sustain themselves. For generations, they held sacred rituals and told stories that helped to define their tribe.

The Chumash believed that there were three worlds: the one on which people lived, the one above it, and one below it. In the lower world lived dangerous and frightening creatures. People inhabited the middle world—a large island surrounded by water. This middle world was held up by two huge serpents. When these serpents became tired and moved, they triggered earthquakes. In the world above, there lived the powerful Sky People who brought good and evil to the middle world.

Here is a story about how the Sky People created the first human beings:

> Long ago, there was a great flood. After this flood, Coyote and Eagle, who lived in the sky, and Sun, Moon, and Morning Star talked about making the first human beings. Night after night, Coyote and Eagle argued whether these people should have hands like Coyote. Lizard only listened. Coyote declared that the people should all be made in his image since he had the finest hands.
>
> At last, Coyote got his way, and everyone agreed that people would have hands like

those of Coyote. The next day, they gathered around a beautiful white rock in the sky. The rock was symmetrical and flat on top. The rock also had such a fine texture that whatever touched it left an exact impression.

Coyote was just about to place his hand on the rock when Lizard quickly reached out and placed his own hand on the rock. A perfect imprint of Lizard's hand remained on the smooth surface. Enraged, Coyote chased Lizard and tried to kill him, but Lizard escaped by skittering down into a deep ravine.

Eagle and Sun approved of the impression made by Lizard, and Coyote could do nothing to change it. It is said that the impression is still on that rock in the sky, and people now have hands like those of Lizard. If Lizard had not made that print, people would today have paws like those of Coyote.

The Chumash considered sacred their climate, environment, and animals that they encountered in daily life. Their traditions and storytelling reflect their **reverence** for the natural world. These values also influenced the development of their societal structure.

The Chumash built homes similar to this reconstructed one.

CHAPTER TWO

Brother, we're getting stronger.

—Georgina Sanchez,
Chumash elder

BUILDING A CIVILIZATION

While the Chumash network was vast and varied in terms of locale and geography, the daily life of the Chumash was centered in the village. There is evidence that there may have been as many as one hundred villages stretched out over their ancestral territory. Villages ranged in size. Some were large enough to be considered towns by today's standards, while others were composed

The Chumash settled in areas close to freshwater sources, such as rivers, lakes, and streams.

The People and Culture of the Chumash

of only a few dwellings and a handful of people. The largest settlements were situated along the Santa Barbara Channel. These villages served as capitals and trading centers for the Island and Interior Chumash who lived in less populated areas. Villages were generally located on high ground. Several key factors determined whether a stretch of land was ideal for inhabitance. First, a freshwater source such as a stream or spring should be nearby. Second, a marsh where the reeds of the bulrush, known as **tule**, should be accessible in order to thatch houses. Finally, there also had to be good beaches for launching and landing numerous canoes, which they used to travel along the waters and between islands.

Rights and Rules

Each village had traditional rights to certain territories for hunting, fishing, and gathering. Many of these areas were near the community, but in some cases, people made long, seasonal journeys to places far from their

The People and Culture of the Chumash

The Chumash and other Native American tribes living in California traded with each other for goods such as jewelry, tools, and clothing.

homes. They set up a temporary camp and worked there for a few days or weeks. Then they returned to their village with baskets laden with food.

Two villages might argue about rights to certain lands. Such disputes were usually settled by a ritual battle. To resolve most conflicts, the Chumash engaged in ritual battles in which the opponents lined up facing each other. Taking turns, one man from each side shot an arrow at the opposing side. When one or perhaps several men were killed, the battle was considered over. Leaders often managed to resolve quarrels through negotiations, with no one getting injured or killed. Villagers sometimes had to defend themselves from attack or went to war to drive intruders from their territory. Other times, they avenged insults such as the refusal of a chief to accept an invitation to a feast or dance. However, every military venture

A typical Chumash dwelling was built with poles and thatched tule or other brush from nature.

The People and Culture of the Chumash

sweathouses primarily to cleanse their bodies and spirits. However, if a hunter was preparing to stalk deer and other game, herbs were sometimes burned to mask his scent. Large sweathouses also served as meeting places for the men. Occasionally, women and children used the sweathouses to treat illnesses and participate in ceremonies.

Other village buildings included storehouses, which were often placed near the houses. Large amounts of food were kept in a big storehouse near the chief's house. The chief needed a generous supply of food because he often had to entertain people and provide for the needy. Each village also had a smooth, level field where contests, such as shinny, kick ball, and hoop-and-pole, and ball games were held. The field, referred to as *malamtepupi*, was often surrounded by a low wall.

A village also had a dance ground for religious ceremonies. Within the dance ground was the **siliyik**. The siliyik consisted of a semicircular area enclosed by a high fence of tule mats. Here priests and **shamans** conducted rituals. Outside the siliyik, people sat around campfires where they were sheltered by a tule-mat windbreak.

The People and Culture of the Chumash

Some Chumash villages had designated areas where ball games would be played. This is one such example.

At work areas, people chipped stone tools and weapons, built canoes, wove baskets, and pounded acorns. There was also a cemetery for burials.

The houses and other structures were loosely situated along a main street. In larger villages, houses were arranged in rows, with paths running like streets between them. Paths led from one house to another, as well as to the common areas. The Chumash lives were centered around family, friends, and work. They lived peacefully and labored hard to provide for themselves, practice their religion, and enjoy games and stories.

Societal Structure

The Chumash did not have a single ruler for the entire people. Each village was led by a chief called a **wot** (rhymes with "boat"). The wot inherited his position from his father and other male ancestors, or he became the leader due to his wealth and influence. Occasionally, women became wots. Some communities had more than one chief, who were most likely the heads of prominent families. Larger villages, such as Syukhtun, which was located at the site of Santa Barbara, and Shisholop, which was situated at the present-day city of Ventura, usually had three or four leaders, one of whom served as head chief. The wots granted hunting and fishing rights, managed hunting and gathering activities, oversaw religious ceremonies, and in rare instances, led the men of the village into battle. Wots made sure that enough food was set aside for religious and social celebrations. Among their most important duties was to ensure the care of the poor and the elderly in the community.

Some areas of Chumash territory were politically organized into an alliance of several villages. The village leaders then formed a regional council, and one was selected as *paqwot*, or head chief. The head chief's assistant, known as the **paha**, managed major religious ceremonies, such as the acorn harvest festival in the autumn and the Winter **Solstice** Ceremony.

Charlie Cooke, or Tiq Slo'w, was a prominent chief of the Chumash. He died in September 2013.

The Chumash community was further organized into three social classes: artisans, shamans, and relatives of the wot. The artisans formed guilds to carry on their various trades. Shamans, who were responsible for the spiritual and physical welfare of the people, cured illnesses and injuries, interpreted dreams, and guided vision quests. The third class was composed of the people who were related to the wot. Other notable people were special messengers of the leaders known as the ksen. The messengers traveled from village to village, making announcements and gathering news.

Another key group was the prestigious **'antap** society. Members of this secret society sang and danced at ceremonies and served as advisors to the wot. Only people from upper-class families could join this secret society, which included the wot, members of the wot's family, shamans, the village paha, and other officials. The 'antap held special ceremonies to ensure a balance in the universe. It arranged the key activities, such as the gathering, storage, and distribution of food, that ensured the well-being of the community. The 'antap also forecast weather, named children, and determined the dates and locations of important ceremonies.

Chumash society was organized into clans named for animals such as the bear, eagle, or coyote. Clan members considered themselves to be related to a common ancestor. Each clan was responsible for certain duties relating to government, sustenance, and rituals. For example, like the eagle, the leader of the animals, members of the Eagle clan were most likely to be wots. Clans were also ranked according to their prestige. The Eagle, Bear, and Snow Goose Clans were more highly

The People and Culture of the Chumash

regarded than the Coyote, Raven, and Dog Clans. Children were born into their mother's clan. Members of different clans lived in the same village, but loyalty to the village was more important than clan membership. People painted their bodies with distinct styles to indicate the village where they lived.

While the Chumash separated themselves by class and clan, their primary allegiance was to their village. The focus on the village as the most important building block of Chumash society influenced the role each villager played in their civilization. These individual roles and dedication to the prosperity of the whole dictated the experience of life within the village.

A Chumash mother holds her child.

The tomol is like a flower on the surface of the ocean.

—Marcus Lopez, Co-Chair of the Barbareño Chumash Council of Santa Barbara

LIFE IN A CHUMASH VILLAGE

Like the majority of early societies, the focus of life in the Chumash village was survival. However, their knowledge of their bountiful landscape allowed them access to the abundant resources of both the land and sea. As a result, the Chumash were not only expert survivalists but also **adept** craftsmen. They built a tradition of constructing materials that honored both function and **aesthetics**. From hunting and gathering to boatbuilding and basket weaving, the Chumash displayed a deep enthusiasm for life in the village.

It Takes a Village

The survival of the Chumash depended on villagers working every day to provide themselves with food, clothing, and shelter. It was typically the men who ventured from their villages to hunt game in the mountains or fish the sea. Women and children dug roots and gathered berries in the meadows and forests. During the cycle of days and seasons, villagers experienced the key events of life—birth, childhood, coming-of-age, marriage, and death. For each occasion, they observed time-honored customs and rituals.

Being Born

The Chumash loved their children and looked forward to the birth of a new baby. When a woman was about to have her child, she made a hole in the ground wherever she happened to be at that time. The hole was warmed by a fire and then lined with clean straw. Here, she delivered her baby, often with the assistance of an older woman. After giving birth, the mother bathed herself in cold water.

Children

The Chumash were gentle people who were rarely angry with their children. Encouraged to behave themselves, children were seldom punished. As they grew up, boys and girls learned their roles in the village and the skills they would need to survive as adults. Girls learned to gather food, cook meals, care for children, and manage the household. Their mother and other women instructed them in handicrafts, such as basket making. Boys learned to hunt and fish and to defend themselves against enemies. They learned various crafts, such as how to make tools and weapons, and were also taught the important roles of governing the village and participating in religious ceremonies.

Maturing

When a young woman had her first period, she was no longer allowed to eat certain foods, such as meat and grease. She also could not gaze into a fire. As boys and girls approached adulthood, they were taken out at night and given a strong drink made from pounded **toloache** root mixed with water. This intoxicating beverage induced visions in which it was believed the young people saw their futures.

Once they had undertaken these rituals and learned to provide for themselves, young women and men were then considered ready to be married.

Strengthening Bonds

Men and women from the same village sometimes married each other. However, people more often chose spouses from other villages. These marriages served to strengthen the bonds among the various communities. People also did not marry within their clan. The men usually offered gifts, such as beads, otter skins, or blankets, to the parents in exchange for permission to marry their daughter. The wedding ceremony often included a lively dance by a man known as "the jealous one." With a pair of pelican wings tied to his head and a bow in his hand, he danced with a woman in a feather cape while another man sang about the wedding night. After a couple was married, they usually lived with the wife's relatives in her village. Only the chief and a few wealthy men could afford more than one wife. Adultery was strictly forbidden and was punished by whipping. Couples generally remained devoted to each other for their entire lives.

Mourning and Honoring the Dead

People mourned the death of loved ones in elaborate funeral ceremonies. The body was carried to a sacred place where a ceremony was held around a large fire. Mourners watched over the body. Then, led by a shaman smoking a pipe, they sang and passed by the body three times. Each time, the mourners lifted the animal skin covering the body and the shaman blew three mouthfuls of smoke over the body. The relatives of the deceased offered beads to the chief, and then the mourners cried out in grief as they proceeded with the body to a cemetery enclosed by a high stockade.

The body was usually buried face down; only the Island Chumash buried their dead face up. The body was laid in a flexed position, with the head to the west. Offerings such as beads, bowls, and weapons were often included in the burial. The cemetery was regarded as sacred ground. Graves were marked with a wooden plank, often painted with black-and-white squares. Sometimes, a pole was raised over the grave from which important objects from the deceased's life

The People and Culture of the Chumash

were hung. These might include the hooks and line of a fisherman or the bows and arrows of a hunter. Sometimes, personal belongings of the deceased or a whale rib, bent like a bow, were laid over the grave.

Survival Without Agriculture

Unlike some Native people, the Chumash did not plant corn or other crops. The Pacific Coast and islands abounded in sources of food. From the sea, they caught over one hundred kinds of fish. They occasionally had to camp while they hunted, fished, or collected plants, but they never had to travel far from their villages to find food. Their settled way of life allowed them more time to pursue artistic endeavors. However, the Chumash who lived in the mountains faced greater challenges in dealing with the rough terrain and in finding game. Each family was responsible for providing for its own members—women gathered while men hunted. However, in some large villages, individuals who became skilled at fishing or handicrafts such as basket making worked in exchange for material objects and food.

The Chumash originally used a throwing spear known as an *atlatl* to hunt elk, deer, and sea mammals. Beginning about 1,500 years ago, they began to use bows and arrows. To catch fish on the open sea and from along the rivers, they used a variety of methods, including dip nets, traps, and baskets. They caught small fish with fishhooks made from abalone and mussel shells. They killed larger fish, seals, sea otters, and porpoises with sharp harpoons. They also used the juice of certain plants to poison the water and stun

RECIPE

ACORN BREAD

INGREDIENTS

1 cup acorn flour

½ cup cornmeal

½ cup wheat flour

1 tablespoon baking soda

1 teaspoon salt

1 cup milk

1 egg, lightly beaten

3 tablespoons vegetable oil

¼ cup honey

Carefully crack and shell dry acorns.

Grind the dry, raw acorns into fine flour with a food processor.

Place one cup of acorn flour in a colander or strainer lined with muslin or coffee filter paper. Put the colander in a sink and run water through the flour to remove all the bitter taste.

The People and Culture of the Chumash

Combine acorn flour with cornmeal, wheat flour, baking soda, and salt. Add milk, egg, honey, and vegetable oil and mix into a moist batter. Pour the batter into a greased pan about 8 inches square and bake at 350 degrees for 20 to 30 minutes.

Makes one 8-inch loaf.

Note: Acorn flour may be dried and stored in sealed plastic bags in a freezer. Acorn flour may also be used in place of regular flour in cookie and pancake recipes.

The Chumash caught wild animals using traps like this one.

The People and Culture of the Chumash

the fish. Along the shore, they gathered clams, mussels, and abalone. They caught crabs in the coastal waters and crayfish in the creeks. Farther inland, men used bows and arrows to hunt mule deer and elk. They used snares and deadfalls to catch rabbits and other small game. They hunted ducks and geese that touched down in the marshes and lakes.

The Chumash ate food from many kinds of wild plants. They harvested berries, nuts, and seeds, most notably acorns from live oak and valley oak trees, the most important food of the Chumash and other Native peoples of California. People also gathered piñon nuts, cherries, and many kinds of roots and bulbs. Foods were prepared and eaten in various ways. Piñon nuts and wild strawberries were eaten raw, while chia seeds were ground into flour. Nuts from the California laurel were roasted and then eaten. Other seeds were toasted and ground to a paste. The Chumash harvested miner's lettuce to use as salad greens. Along the coast, people gathered seaweed, which they chopped and dried in an oven or ate raw or boiled. They ate rose hips fresh from the plant or brewed into tea. The tart, sticky berries of the manzanita shrub were made into cider or preserved as a jelly.

The People and Culture of the Chumash

The Chumash crafted intricately decorated *tomols*, such as this one. They continue the tradition today.

The Chumash used parts of an animal, such as its teeth, to carve tools and weapons.

The Chumash roasted meat and fish over an open fire and cooked shellfish in soups and stews. Acorns required long and laborious preparation. The dried acorns were first shelled and ground to a powder between two stones called a mortar and pestle. Acorns have bitter tannic acid, which had to be thoroughly leached, or washed away, from the flour. The acorn flour was then mixed with water in a tightly woven basket and cooked with heated stones placed in the liquid. Women stirred the mixture as it came to a boil and gradually thickened into a mush. The Chumash enjoyed this thick acorn soup along with fish and meat at every meal.

The House of the Sea

The most striking achievement of the Chumash was their distinctive type of boat, which was called a **tomol**.

The People and Culture of the Chumash

Sturdy and swift, gracefully shaped tomols were used for ocean fishing; for hunting seals, sea lions, and sea otters; and for traveling between the coastal towns. These boats were also crucial to trade between the islands and mainland. In the words of one Chumash man, Fernando Librado (also called Kitsepawit), "The canoe was the 'house of the sea.'" A tomol was worth more than a house, and only a wealthy person could afford to own one. Every prosperous coastal town had several tomols nosed up onto the beach.

Men built tomols with tools made from animal bones, stones, or shells. They worked patiently, taking at least forty days and often from two to six months to complete a tomol. With whalebone or antler wedges, they split logs into rough boards about ¾-inch (1.9 centimeters) thick. They preferred redwood, which swelled when wet to seal the cracks between boards. Redwood does not grow near the beaches, but redwood logs floated as driftwood from the forests of northern California where the trees grew in abundance along the coast. They also used pine and sometimes other driftwood. With shell and stone tools, they scraped the surface of the planks. Starting with a heavy plank for the bottom, they glued three or four rows of planks together, edge to edge, with *yop*, a mixture of hot pitch and asphalt, a kind of tar that washed onto the beaches. These planks formed each side of the tomol. After the yop had dried, holes were drilled in the planks, and the planks were lashed together with twine made from milkweed plants. The holes and seams were sealed with more yop. The surface of the canoe was then smoothed with sandstone and lightly sanded with sharkskin. The craftsmen coated the tomol with a mixture of tar, pine pitch, and red paint to make sure the vessel was completely waterproof. Along with the red paint, the tomol was often decorated with abalone shells. Craftsmen also made two or three long paddles, shaped like a shovel at each end.

Ranging in length from 12 to 30 feet (3.6 to 9 m), a tomol could carry a crew of three or four and a considerable amount of goods. Large canoes could transport twelve people and some as many as twenty people. When finished, the tomol was carried to the edge of the water. The builders offered a prayer and then dragged the canoe through the surf. It was loaded with goods and people, with the captain in the stern, or back. One crew member, usually a young boy or an old man, sat in the middle of the canoe and with a basket or abalone shell bailed water that seeped into the tomol. Quite seaworthy, tomols were known to have been navigated with double-bladed paddles as far as 65 miles (105 km) into the open ocean.

A highly regarded group of men, known as the Brotherhood of the Tomol, knew how to make these distinctive canoes and paddle them across the Santa Barbara Channel. If a young man wanted to learn how to make a tomol, he had to ask if he could join the brotherhood. If approved, he paid a fee and was then accepted as a brother and taught the secrets of the craft. Members of the brotherhood also knew how to ferry island goods, such as stone blades and drills, and fish, such as shark, bonito, and halibut, to the mainland. Every brother helped a brother in times of trouble. Brothers became rich and respected since they could

The People and Culture of the Chumash

travel far out to sea and catch the largest fish. They could also journey great distances and bring back impressive quantities of food, tools, and ornaments. They even traveled as far as Santa Catalina Island, where they traded for highly prized soapstone bowls.

No one is sure how long tomols lasted—it depended on how often they were used and how well they were maintained. The Chumash usually stored their tomols in a moist, shady area until they were needed for a sea journey. Before embarking, they inspected the vessel carefully and made any necessary repairs. If they took good care of their tomol, it would remain seaworthy for many years. Around 1850, the Chumash made the last tomols to be used for fishing and trade expeditions. In 1913, Fernando Librado, then an elderly man, constructed a tomol for anthropologist John P. Harrington, to demonstrate how the canoes were built. When he was younger, Librado had observed the last tomols being built by older men in his village. Since the 1970s, a number of tomols have been made.

A Trade Network

The Chumash were great traders who exchanged a wide variety of goods among themselves and with other Native peoples. They often bartered for goods or used strings of shell beads as money to purchase items. Among the Native peoples of California, the Chumash were the primary source for the shells that were used as money. This money, called 'anchum, was made from various clams and snail shells but most often from the olivella. This shell comes from a marine snail. People living on the Channel Islands, especially those

Shells such as these were carved into beads as well as used as a form of money called 'anchum.

The People and Culture of the Chumash

on Santa Cruz Island, specialized in making the bead money. They served as the mint, or source of currency, for the Chumash living on the mainland. It is believed that the words Chumash and 'anchum are related and that the name Chumash once had something to do with the making of bead money by the Island Chumash. The value of the money depended on the rarity of the shell and the difficulty of manufacture. Beads made from the callus—the thick part of the shell near the opening— were worth twice as much as beads made from the wall of the shell, because fewer beads could be made from the smaller callus. People determined the value of the beads by the rarity of the shell and the length of the strand—according to the number of times it could be wrapped around one's hand. Eight strings of beads are thought to have equaled one Spanish silver dollar.

Deer and rabbits did not live on the islands. So, the Island Chumash paddled to the mainland where they used shell beads to buy rabbit skins, deerskins, and antlers. They also traded their fish, fish oils, sea lion meat, sea otter pelts, whale bones, and other ocean bounty for foods that were scarce on the islands, such as acorns, pine nuts, chia seeds, and wild cherries. The Chumash who lived in the interior valleys journeyed on foot to the coast and traded for shells and beads, asphalt, fish, sea otter pelts, and other goods that they needed. In exchange, Inland Chumash offered black pigment, obsidian, antelope and elk skins, nuts, seeds, and herbs.

The trade network extended beyond the Chumash to other tribes in the region. Black steatite, or soapstone, dug from Santa Catalina Island—to the

Chumash clothing was made from tanned buckskin and was often decorated with shell beads.

painted their bodies, and for special ceremonies, they wore more body paint and jewelry. Ceremonial dancers and singers wore feathered skirts, headdresses, and other elaborate regalia depicting animals or birds. This attire might be made from bearskins, twisted milkweed fiber, or feathers from the California condor.

Function and Elegance

The Chumash were highly regarded craftspeople. The tomol is perhaps the best example of their great skill and artistry. However, they made many other objects. They expertly carved wooden plates, bowls, trays, and boxes. They also used wood for harpoon shafts and other hunting and fishing equipment. The Chumash preferred chert, a kind of flint, and occasionally obsidian for making points for arrows and spears. They also chipped pieces of flint into knives, scrapers, drills, and other tools. They fashioned many other tools and cooking utensils from stone, especially from soapstone, which they carved into bowls, smoking pipes, and arrow-shaft straighteners. They also made beads, ornaments, and animal figures that served as charms. Serpentine, another soft stone, was made into doughnut shapes that were fitted over digging sticks to provide added weight. Sandstone was shaped into bowls used for grinding seeds.

Artisans carved wood and bone into flutes, whistles, and rattles. Bone was also used to make fishhooks, needles, awls, and hairpins. It was made into wedges and gouges for woodworking and into flakers for chipping arrowheads. People who lived along the ocean made stools from the vertebrae of whales. The Chumash fashioned shells into beads, ornaments, and money. Plant fibers were made into houses and clothing. Yucca fibers were made into thick cords for harpoon lines. Fibers of hemp, nettle, and milkweed were twisted into string. The Chumash wove this string into fishnets and bags.

Basket Making

The Chumash are celebrated for their finely woven, carefully decorated baskets. These were needed in almost every area of daily life. Some baskets were made as gifts; others were used in grinding seeds and

Chumash baskets have many different designs and are woven with care.

nuts. Many served as storage containers. Even water was stored in large baskets. Sealed on the inside with asphalt, these baskets could hold up to six gallons of water. People used baskets for gathering, storing, preparing, and serving foods. They kept their money and other valuables in baskets, and measured acorns for trade in baskets. They toted babies in baskets and used baskets for gambling and gifts, as well as in sacred ceremonies. Chumash houses even resembled upside-down baskets.

Basket makers primarily used two weaving techniques, twining and coiling. Women made twined baskets by twisting rush stems or split tule around the rigid warps that radiated like the spokes of a wheel from a central point. Sturdy and practical, twined baskets were used as cradles, leaching basins, sieves, water bottles, and fish traps. The coiled baskets, which began with a spiraling base of three slender rods, were wrapped and sewn together with split rush strands. The Chumash became especially renowned for their lovely coiled work, which was used for trays, bowls of many sizes, and hats.

Most of the baskets were tan in color. Women often wove black designs into them. To obtain the color black, they buried rush stalks in dark mud or soaked them in water tinted with acorns and a piece of iron. Some stalks naturally had a reddish-orange color, and weavers used them to fill in designs or to create a background color. The most popular design was a 1-inch (2.54 cm) band, running as a border below the rim. Beneath this border, baskets were decorated with different geometric patterns, including vertical bars, horizontal bands, zigzags, stepped lines, and an intricate network of lines. Several of these designs were so commonly used that they acquired popular names, such as Little Deer, Points, Butterfly, and Arms. Among some people, Arms was known as Auail Plumes. The Chumash rarely wove figures of humans or animals into their baskets. They often finished a basket by what is called rim ticking, or sewing little blocks of alternating dark and light stitches on the basket.

Coiled baskets could be tight enough to hold water. Women could boil water or cook soup in these baskets by placing heated rocks in them. Twined basketry bottles were less tightly woven than coiled baskets. However, they were often coated on the inside with asphalt to make them watertight. Women first powdered the hard tar and placed it into the finished bottle along with small, heated stones. They shook and turned the basket until the asphalt had melted and evenly coated the inside. Dumping out the rocks, they filled the basket with water. The basket was cured overnight, after which it was ready to be refilled with fresh water.

The Chumash traded baskets to other Native peoples long before the Spanish ventured into California. The Spanish greatly admired the baskets and sent them home as gifts to family and friends. During the **mission** period, a number of remarkable baskets, including ones with coin designs and Spanish words with more than 220 stitches per square inch, were intricately woven. Despite the devastating impact of the Spanish, Mexicans, and Americans on their traditional way of life, the Chumash continued to make

The People and Culture of the Chumash

impressive baskets until the last of the great weavers died around 1915.

Today, about four hundred Chumash baskets have survived. Most are housed in museums and private collections around the world, such as the Smithsonian Institution and the Santa Barbara Museum of Natural History. Fortunately, contemporary weavers have carefully studied many of these baskets and John P. Harrington's early interviews with basket makers. They have learned to work with the wild plant materials and to again make traditional Chumash baskets. These baskets are a source of inspiration for a new generation of Chumash weavers whose dedication ensures that this art form will flourish well into the future.

While the coastal environment determined many aspects of life in the Chumash village, the expert manipulation of the land's offerings allowed villages to flourish. From the construction of the tomol to their expert basket making, Chumash people became masters of the natural world that they revered.

Many Chumash beliefs
are rooted in nature.

*I don't believe in magic.
I believe in the sun and
the stars, the water, the
tides, the floods, the owls,
the hawks flying, the river
running, the wind talking
... Because we and they
are the same.*

—Billy Frank, Jr.,
Chumash elder

BELIEFS OF THE CHUMASH

Spiritual beliefs deeply influenced Chumash life. These beliefs, passed down through storytelling and dance, birthed a variety of customs and rituals that shaped the life experience of Chumash people.

The Universe and Origins

The Chumash believed that the universe was composed of three worlds layered upon each other like flat, circular trays. The middle world was the earth, or the "World of the People." In the world above lived powerful beings, including the Sun, Moon, Morning Star, and the other Sky People. In the lower world lived dangerous creatures, known as *nunashish*, who rose to the middle world at night and frightened anyone who encountered them.

The Chumash believed that long ago, before there were humans, an earlier people known as the First People inhabited the middle world. These First People lived much like the Chumash, but there was a great flood, and most of the First People were turned into animals, plants, and natural forces, such as thunder. Some of the First People escaped by ascending into the sky where they became the Sky People. A council of the Sky People led to the creation of humans, and the Sky People were revered as the most powerful beings in the universe. Like humans, they had intelligence and emotion, and they often acted unpredictably to bring good or evil. For example, Sun brought warmth but could also make the earth too hot or seemingly vanish so that cold weather swept over the land. The Chumash were so fascinated by the night sky that shamans also served as astronomers who could explain the workings of the universe to their people. The Chumash likely saw a relationship between the afterlife and the universe. In one story, a dead woman encountered many obstacles as she journeyed along a path through the Milky Way.

The Chumash also believed that all human and supernatural beings sought to gain more power over good and evil. To do so, the person practiced secret rituals through which he called upon a dream helper.

The People and Culture of the Chumash

The helper could be an animal, plant, insect, distant star, planet, or a natural force such as thunder. Among the most important helpers were Bear, Eagle, Beaver, Thunder, and Whirlwind. Dream helpers could be called upon to assist with basket making, a long canoe journey, or gambling, or in times of peril from enemy attack or natural disaster.

Vision Quests, Guides, and Medicines

To acquire a dream helper, one went on a vision quest. With the aid of a shaman, the seeker fasted and drank toloache. This dangerous drink was consumed in the belief that it allowed an individual to directly appeal to a dream helper. If a dream helper appeared in the vision, the seeker then made a talisman known as an *'atishwin* that represented the helper. Thereafter, the talisman was carefully protected. Misfortune befell the person who allowed the 'atishwin to be lost or stolen. Shamans, chiefs, and other prominent individuals often had more than one dream helper, an indication of their great power in the village. By contrast, those who had no dream helper were regarded as frightened, helpless, and easily dominated by more powerful individuals.

Spiritual guidance was provided by the shamans. It was believed that shamans received their power from a spirit who appeared to them in a vision. Wearing bearskin garments and belts hung with deer hooves, shamans acted as doctors who believed that sickness was caused by a patient's spiritual problems. They cured injuries and illness with ritual songs, dances, and prayers, herbal medicines, and polished stone charms. Shamans also used a hollow tube for blowing away

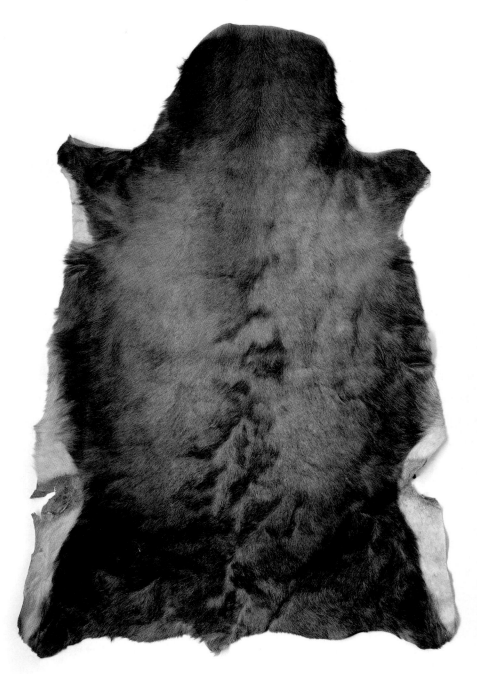

The Chumash wore animal furs to keep warm in cold winter months.

The People and Culture of the Chumash

or sucking out a patient's evil spirits. The patient was cured once an object was supposedly removed from the body, although the object was a stone or small animal that the shaman had actually brought with him.

To treat various maladies, the Chumash used nearly one hundred medicines obtained from the bark, roots, and flowers of various plants. Nettle was used to ease rheumatism and paralysis. The shaman made a bed of cut stalks on which the patient would lie and vigorously roll around. Or the shaman beat the patient with a handful of nettle stalks. The Chumash used willow bark for sore throats and elder flowers for colds. Poison oak was even used to dress wounds. One of their favorite medicines was chuchupate, a root of a plant in the carrot family that grew high in the mountains. People chewed chuchupate to give themselves strength and to ward off illness. They also mixed animal fat with ground minerals and painted it on the patient. Seawater was sometimes drunk to cleanse the digestive system. Another treatment required the patient to swallow live red ants.

A Tradition of Dance and Song

The Chumash frequently held sacred rituals in their villages at which they danced and sang. They held a mourning ceremony when a person died and gathered to celebrate weddings and induct a new chief. At times, people from several villages came together for a major ceremony. The two most significant ceremonies honored Earth and the sun.

A thanksgiving festival, the Hutash Ceremony, honored the earth goddess, known as Shup or Hutash.

She provided the Chumash with food. It was held in late summer or early autumn after the acorn harvest and in major communities such as Muwu, Shisholop, and Syukhtun. People came from miles away, including the Channel Islands, for this large gathering that lasted for five or six days. Spectators sat on tule mats around a sacred area where performers sang and danced. Visiting chiefs sat in special locations marked by painted poles. In the siliyik, unseen by others, two old men blew ceremonial whistles.

On December 21—the shortest day of the year—the Chumash attended the Winter Solstice Ceremony to honor the sun. On the first day, all debts from the last year had to be settled. The next day, the paha, who was regarded as the image of the sun, and twelve assistants, who were considered rays of the sun, set up a pole called the Sunstick. About 16 inches (41 cm) long, the Sunstick had a stone disk on top. This disk was painted with twelve sun rays. These rays were aligned with the sun to cast a circular shadow. With the powerful Sunstick, the paha symbolically drew the sun back toward the earth to ensure the cycle of the seasons and the growth of plants in the ensuing year.

In all of their ceremonies, the Chumash participated in dances, many of which were social while others were deeply religious. Both men and women danced to the music of flutes, whistles, and occasionally the scattering of seeds. Many dances honored land animals, including the California condor, bear, beaver, fox, coyote, and blackbird. There were also dances for ocean creatures, such as the killer whale, swordfish, and barracuda, and even a seaweed dance. The dancers wore elaborate

The Chumash used a sun stick, like this one, for ceremonies and other special occasions. Photo by Ken Lee.

regalia in which they represented the animal or plant. The performers also adorned themselves with body paint for each of the dances.

The Swordfish Dance was one of the most important rituals. The dancer wore either a swordfish skull inlaid with pieces of shell or a headdress that represented the fish's sword. Offerings of beads and other gifts were made to the swordfish, believed to be the chief of all the sea animals.

The Chumash enjoyed many kinds of songs, including lullabies, gambling songs, songs of joy, storytelling songs, and songs for curing the sick.

These cave drawings were created by ancient Chumash members.

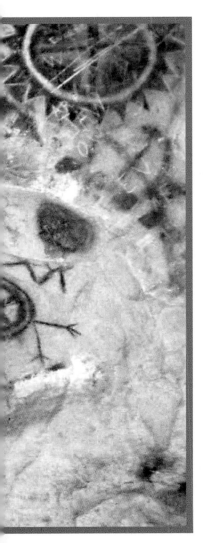

Songs were part of the ceremonial dances and were often accompanied by musical instruments. The most important musical instrument was the wansak', or clapper stick, which was made from a partially split elderberry stick. This wooden instrument was played by striking it against the hand to make a clapping sound or by shaking it to make a quick, rattling noise. The clapper stick was used to keep the beat or rhythm of a song or dance. Other popular musical instruments included deer-bone flutes, bird-bone whistles, and rattles made from turtle shells with small pebbles inside.

Prayer Through Painting

The Chumash created strikingly beautiful, yet mysterious rock paintings, or **pictographs**, in hundreds of caves throughout their homeland. Although these rock paintings were often exquisite, they were not made as art. Hidden away in secret places, they were not intended for public viewing. It is believed that they were made during toloache rites. Shamans most likely painted the cryptic symbols as a means of asking spiritual powers for help in the daily lives of the Chumash. The colorful and complex paintings depicted a variety of figures, including abstract beings resembling birds and fish. Others featured stars and planets, mythic figures, natural forces, and abstract designs. Many of the symbols represented fertility, water, and rain. The circle and a curved line split on the ends were two of the common themes in many paintings.

The pigments for making the paints came from different kinds of minerals. By crushing colored rocks into a fine powder, artists obtained red, blue, yellow, green, brown, gray, and white pigments. Red was obtained from hematite. White came from gypsum or a very fine powder called diatomaceous earth. Black was derived from charcoal or manganese oxide. These minerals were ground and mixed with a liquid binder, usually water, animal fat, or milkweed sap. The Chumash applied this heavy paint with brushes of soap plant, yucca, or animal tails. Sometimes, they painted with their fingers. Dry lumps of pigment were also used like chalk to draw lines.

The majority of the paintings were made on sandstone in rock shelters and caves in valleys and canyons. Paintings with the most varied and **enigmatic** symbols were usually created in remote caves. Most of the paintings were made in the mountains. Many rock paintings are believed to be less than one thousand years old, and some are fairly recent. At Painted Cave, for example, complex designs have been painted at various times, often over earlier paintings. It is believed that one painting depicts a solar eclipse that occurred on November 24, 1677. Other figures were made before and after that event, in styles that changed over time.

Rock paintings are held sacred by Chumash today, and the locations of many are kept secret.

Communal Gaming

The Chumash enjoyed competitive games, and they usually gambled on the outcome. They did not believe in luck but thought that winning or losing the wager was influenced by supernatural powers. Every village had an area, known as a malamtepupi, that was set aside for games. The smooth, level ground was sometimes bordered by a low wall. People played other games, such as dice with walnut shells or sticks. Children enjoyed bear tag in which everyone ran from the "bear" who was "it." Boys and young men liked to play hoop-and-pole, or payas, with a hoop made from a willow stem wrapped in buckskin. Four or five inches (10 or 12 cm) in diameter, the hoop was rolled along the ground in a straight line. Standing to one side about twelve feet away, a contestant waited. As the hoop rolled by he threw a 6-foot (1.8 m) wooden pole like a spear. If he speared the hoop, he scored one point. Sometimes, players shot an arrow at the hoop. Two or more players could compete in this game. The first player to score twelve points won the game.

The Chumash also played the hand game 'alewsa, with two teams of two or more players on each side. The players of one team had two sticks or bones—one black and one white. They all hid the sticks in their hands, which they held in front of themselves. The object of the game was for the opponents to guess which player held the white stick. The opposing team had a "killer" who made the guess for his team. If he guessed correctly, his team received a counter stick. His team then hid the painted sticks. The game was played until all the counter sticks—as many as fifteen—were won by one side. The hand game is still popular among the Chumash and other Native people in California.

One of the most popular team sports among the Chumash was shinny, or *tikauwich*. During major ceremonies, nearly everyone in two competing villages might play against each other, with as many as two or three hundred contestants on the field. The square field could be as long as 300 yards (274 m) on each side and had goalposts at opposite ends. The players carried shinny sticks, which resembled hockey sticks. The object of the game was to hit the small wooden ball through the opponent's goalpost. Shinny formed the foundation of what is now known as lacrosse. These games were hotly contested. Women rarely got into fights, but the men frequently brawled. The Ventureño Chumash were reputed to be the best shinny players. It was customary for the winning team to give half of its winnings in bets to the chief of the village hosting the celebration. This contribution helped to pay for the costs of the event.

An Oral Tradition

Among the Chumash, stories were passed down from one generation to the next. In the evenings, children gathered around the fire to listen to one of their elders. They not only enjoyed these stories but also learned about their history and traditions through them. Some stories were humorous, while others explained the mysteries of the universe, the land, the waters, and the

The Chumash played many games. One such game involved a ball and stick.

Alan Salazar, a modern-day Chumash storyteller, wears a coyote hat to help him tell a story involving the character Coyote.

The People and Culture of the Chumash

night sky. Stories, such as "The Sky People," described the actions of Coyote and other supernatural beings:

There is a place above where Sun, Morning Star, Coyote, and Eagle play the gambling game, peon. There are two players on each side and Moon is the referee. They gather in a special house where only peon can be played. They play every night for a year, staying up until dawn. Coyote likes to bet on the outcome.

On Christmas Eve they count the counter sticks to determine which side won. If Eagle's side comes out ahead, there will be a rainy year. Sun wagers many kinds of food—acorns, deer, wild cherries, seeds, ducks, and geese. If Sun loses, Coyote can hardly wait to receive his payment. He pulls open the door and all his winnings fall to the earth, so that that year people will have plenty of food.

However, if Sun wins, Coyote pays him with human lives. Coyote always wants to give old people to him, and Sun squabbles with him. Occasionally, Sun wins the argument and gets to choose a young person to die.

Every day, the Sky People have a particular task. Morning Star shines at dawn, Sun lights the day, and Moon illuminates the night. Moon is a single woman with a house near Sun's house. Moon and Sun never age: they are always there.

·JVAN·R·CABRILLO·

Spanish explorer Juan
Cabrillo arrived in
California in the 1540s.

1542

CHAPTER FIVE

Our language is a sleeping tiger just waiting to rise.

—Ernestine De Soto

OVERCOMING HARDSHIPS

Chumash culture thrived for centuries prior to the arrival of foreign explorers. Like many other Native people, at first the Chumash welcomed the European visitors with gifts and celebration. Chumash culture continued to prosper for hundreds of years after the first encounters with Europeans, but eventually their way of life was threatened and almost totally annihilated by foreign disease, warfare, enslavement, and **colonialism**.

Encountering Europeans

In 1542, the Chumash first came into contact with Europeans when the Portuguese commander Juan Rodríguez Cabrillo guided a fleet of Spanish ships along the California coast. He may have been searching for a sea route to China, but he was greeted by the Chumash. The friendly Chumash, who were the first California natives to encounter Europeans, paddled out to the ships in boats laden with gifts. Despite the hospitality, Cabrillo claimed all the lands of the Chumash for Spain. In 1602, Spanish explorer Sebastián Vizcaíno sailed into the bay that he named Santa Barbara in honor of Saint Barbara's day. Chumash relations with the newcomers remained friendly, even when the Spanish began to use the Santa Barbara Channel as a stopover on voyages across the Pacific Ocean. The Spanish had not yet established a settlement there, and the Chumash continued to thrive for the next 160 years with little direct intrusion from the Europeans.

Europeans did not drastically influence the Chumash way of life until the 1770s, when the Spanish began to build missions and forts known as presidios in their territory. The Spanish, who had established an empire in Mexico and South America, believed that they had to protect California from the Russians and the English, who were exploring and trading along the northwest coast. In 1769, Gaspar de Portolá led an expedition to establish missions and presidios in California. In a joint military and religious effort, the soldiers were to protect the settlements while Franciscan priests, known as

The People and Culture of the Chumash

An engraving of Sebastián Vizcaíno

padres in Spanish, pacified and converted the Natives. At this time, Portolá journeyed among the Chumash, reported that they were friendly, and offered gifts of

One of the missions the Chumash came to live in and work at was Mission Santa Barbara.

The Santa Barbara Mission, Cal.

baskets, fish, seeds, and acorns. However, the Spanish intended to use the Chumash and other California Natives as slave laborers to enrich their empire. Although many of the missionaries hoped to better the lives of the Chumash, some were very cruel. Whatever the priests' motives, the traditional life of the Chumash

The People and Culture of the Chumash

began to be destroyed when the missions were established in their homeland.

In 1772, the Spanish established San Luis Obispo, the first of the five missions in Chumash territory: San Luis Obispo, San Buenaventura (at Ventura), Santa Barbara, La Purísima Concepcíon (near Lompoc), and Santa Inés. Completed in 1804, Santa Inés was the last of the missions to be built on Chumash land. The priests hoped to convert the Natives to Christianity. The Chumash were lured to the missions by attractive trade beads. Some terrified people fled to the missions after a major earthquake in 1812. Many Chumash on the Channel Islands were slaughtered by Russian whalers, and the survivors made their way to the missions. They willingly adapted to a new way of life as farmers, craftsmen, and Christians. However, most were forced to work on the missions. Eventually, their villages declined so much that it was impossible to survive in traditional communities, and most Chumash people had to enter the mission system.

Mission Life

Once the Chumash had been baptized, they were regarded as neophytes, or new converts. According to Spanish law, neophytes had to abandon their villages and live near the mission. At the age of five or six, children of the neophytes were taken from their parents and forced to live in dormitories. They had to attend religious services conducted in Spanish and their own Native language. The Chumash also had to give up their traditional dress and wear woolen clothing made at the mission. Children learned farming, carpentry, masonry, ironworking, pottery, weaving, and other crafts. Hunting, fishing, and gathering were abandoned in favor of agriculture and trades. People worked without pay. Instead of dome-shaped tule houses, they now lived in rectangular **adobe** rooms. Though ravaged by this mistreatment, the peaceful Chumash did not openly resist any of these regulations. To do otherwise would risk severe punishment—beatings, imprisonment, and backbreaking labor.

Although the Chumash had initially welcomed the Spanish, they suffered terribly under their harsh rule. But the Chumash and the other Native California peoples were even more devastated by smallpox, measles, and other European diseases that swept through the missions. They had little or no resistance to these diseases, and young children were especially susceptible. The worst was a measles epidemic in the

The People and Culture of the Chumash

The Chumash held many roles in the mission. The Chumash musicians pictured here played at Mission San Buenaventura, circa 1873.

winter of 1806, which killed many people along the California coast. Alcoholism soon became a devastating problem for California Natives, including the Chumash. The population of the Chumash went into sharp decline once the Spanish arrived.

When the Mexican government, which had won independence from Spain in 1821, took control of California, the missions were severely hampered by a lack of supplies. The Chumash rebelled against the mission system at Santa Inés, La Purísima, and Santa Barbara in 1824. Neophytes from Santa Barbara and Santa Inés then abandoned their missions and joined with the rebels at La Purísima. The Chumash held the mission for more than a month, but surrendered when confronted by troops equipped with cannons. Some

Chumash fled to the mountains and others sought refuge among the Yokuts and other Native people living farther inland. However, the revolts quickly ended, and many Chumash returned to the missions.

In 1833, the Mexican government began to dismantle the missions, and the vast land holdings passed from the Catholic Church to Mexican landowners. The Mexicans freed the Chumash and promised to return a portion of their lands. However, the Chumash never received any of their former territory. The missions no longer provided a livelihood, and ancestral Chumash lands were now owned by wealthy Mexicans. A few people tried farming for themselves, but they were driven from the land and enslaved by the settlers who were pouring into the territory from Mexico. Many worked long hours as servants or ranch hands for little or no wages on large ranches. A few people sought work in Los Angeles and the other towns growing along the coast, and some fled to the interior to live with the Yokuts and the Kitanemuk.

Struggles to Survive

Within a few decades, the Chumash were nearly wiped out. By 1839, only about 250 Native people remained at Santa Barbara Mission.

In 1848, Mexico ceded California to the United States, and Americans seized the last of Chumash lands. Gold was discovered in northern California, and thousands of settlers poured into California, hoping to get rich not only as gold prospectors but also as farmers, ranchers, and merchants. Even more settlers

The People and Culture of the Chumash

arrived after California became a state in 1850. The newcomers either feared or pitied the impoverished Chumash. There were no laws to protect the Chumash, and they were driven from their few remaining villages. People scattered throughout the region, afraid to admit that they were Chumash. As Chumash children learned Spanish and English, the Chumash languages were abandoned. Unable to find jobs, many lived in poverty, outcasts in their own land.

Despite these many hardships, a few Chumash struggled to preserve some remnants of their traditional life. Wots were still selected as late as 1862 when Pomposa, a Chumash woman, became chief of the Ventura at the town of Saticoy. In 1869, she gave the last traditional ceremony. Fernando Librado, who spent most of his early years at San Buenaventura Mission, devoted most of his life to learning about Chumash traditions, handicrafts, stories, and songs. He visited many elders and tried to learn as much as possible about traditional beliefs and practices. When he was an old man, Fernando shared much of this knowledge with John P. Harrington, who preserved these traditions through various writings.

One Chumash community did manage to survive the challenges of change. In 1855, the US government set aside a parcel of 120 acres (48.5 hectares) for a little more than one hundred Chumash people living near the Santa Inés Mission. This land became the only reservation for the Chumash. Officially known as the Santa Ynez Chumash Reservation, this reservation was reduced in size in 1901, becoming the smallest in California. Most of the few remaining Chumash lived in Ventura or Santa Barbara, or on ranches where they worked as shepherds, cowboys, laborers, or servants.

An Endangered Language

California had the greatest number of languages of any region in North America. Chumash, or Chumashan, though possibly related to some of the other California languages, is now considered a language family all to itself, including at least six separate languages: Ventureño, Barbareño, Ynezeño (also written Ineseño, called Samala), Purisimeño, Obispeño, and Island Chumash. Because the groups speaking these languages lived in relative isolation from each other for thousands of years, distinct languages developed. Members of each group could not understand the language of any of its neighbors.

The Spanish nearly wiped out the Chumash by the early 1800s. When the United States took over California, English gradually replaced the Native languages. By the beginning of the twentieth century, Spanish or English was spoken in most California households. Throughout the early to mid-1900s, children learned English in public schools. Only a few individuals learned their Native languages as they grew up. Those born before 1900 remembered their own language, but it vanished as their elders passed away. The last known Native speaker of Barbareño, Mary J. Yee, died in 1964.

Here are some examples of the Barbareño Chumash language based on *An Interim Barbareño Chumash Dictionary* as spoken by Mary Yee and compiled by

Kenneth W. Whistler in 1980. Chumash is complex, and the following examples have been simplified. The vowels and the consonants may be pronounced as in English. Chumash pronunciation includes the glottal stop, a catch-in-the-breath expression, similar to the stop in "uh-oh." A glottal stop is indicated by an apostrophe (').

People and Daily Life

'ixpanish	acorn
ya'	arrow
ha'wa	aunt
'a'mi	brother, older
tomol	canoe
paha	ceremony leader
wot'	chief
ch'ish'i	child
sha'y	daughter
kiwa'nan	good-bye
'u'nu	grandchild
nono	grandfather
ne'ne	grandmother
haku	hello
'ap	house
'ihi'y	man
ksen	messenger
'antap	religious society
siliyik	sacred enclosure
'a'lalexpech	singer
'amut'ey	sister

'a'mi	sister, older
wop	son
'atashwin	talisman
tat'a	uncle
'eneq	woman

Parts of the Body

pu, wach'ax	arm
tu'	ear
shipuk	elbow
tiq	eye
mimi	finger, toe
'i'l, 'eqe'ne	foot
pu	hand
noqsh, 'oqwo'n	head
'ayapis, 'antik, ahash	heart
istukun	knee
qe'nen	shoulder
pax	skin

Natural World

muhuw, xasxas'	beach
shi	cliff
'enemes, naxalamuw	island
squnt'aw	lightning
shup	land
muhuw, pana'yi'w	shore
'alapay	sky
'aqiwo	star
'alishaw	sun
stawayik'	valley

The People and Culture of the Chumash

Although there are no first-language speakers of any Chumash language alive today, there are multiple efforts being made to revive Chumash language and culture. In 1978, Dr. Richard Applegate did his PhD dissertation on Ineseño grammar at the University of California, Berkeley. Since then, he has dedicated his career to helping Chumash elders educate descendants. He collaborated with the Santa Inez Chumash Education Committee to create a ten-week language program that teaches students to speak, read, and write the language of Chumash ancestors. In 2007, they successfully published *The Samala-English Dictionary: A Guide to the Samala Language of the Ineseño Chumash People.* The groundbreaking dictionary includes over four thousand entries and a pronunciation guide.

Efforts are being made to revive the Purisimeño language as well. In 2015, the Western Institute for Endangered Language Documentation (WIELD) compiled the Purisimeño-English Lexicon (Preliminary Edition). The **lexicon** is based in part on the work of J.P. Harrington, a well-known **linguist** who mentored Dr. Applegate. While the text is not being used for **pedagogy**, it is a tool for linguists to analyze this endangered language.

Though European settlers sought to **eradicate** the Chumash way of life, they were unsuccessful. Historically, the Chumash have suffered catastrophic losses to their people and culture, but today they are committed to preserving their way of life through a variety of cultural events and education programs.

Today the Chumash remain a vital part of California's history, despite suffering decades of hardship.

CHAPTER SIX

The story of the Santa Ynez Band of Chumash is a story of hope, optimism, and success. We are looking ahead for the well-being of the next generations as we honor our heritage and traditions today.

—Kenneth Kahn, Tribal Chairman

THE NATION'S PRESENCE NOW

After the introduction of European colonialism, the Chumash struggled to keep their culture. The increasing pressure to **assimilate** and abandon their previous way of living was extraordinary, but the Chumash that remain today are proud of their heritage. They are committed to preserving a vibrant culture that honors their ancestors and educates the world on the Chumash way of life.

Adapting to New Lifestyles

By the beginning of the twentieth century, every Chumash village except one had been abandoned. Somehow, a small group of Chumash managed to survive as a community along Zanja de Cota Creek near Santa Inés Mission. In 1855, the United States granted land to the Chumash living in this area, and in 1901, the government formally established a reservation here. Although the reservation is small, it is now the home of the only federally recognized Chumash tribe in the United States. Only those people living at Zanja de Cota were allowed to enroll as members of the tribe at Santa Ynez. The remaining Chumash lived alone or in small families in Ventura, Santa Barbara, and San Luis Obispo Counties in southern California.

By the early 1900s, most Chumash were of mixed ancestry because of intermarriage with other California Natives, and with Mexicans, Mexican-Americans, and Americans. Over the past generations, the number of Chumash has steadily grown. Compiled between 1968 and 1972, the California Indian Judgment Roll listed 1,925 people as Chumash. Of these people, 865 were then living in the three counties that once comprised most of Chumash territory. It is estimated that there are now as many as five thousand Chumash people living in the United States.

The 1940 census of the Santa Ynez Reservation, used to determine the voting membership, counted just over 150 people. Chumash descendants must have at least one-fourth "degree of blood" to become tribal members. Since 1977, Housing and Urban

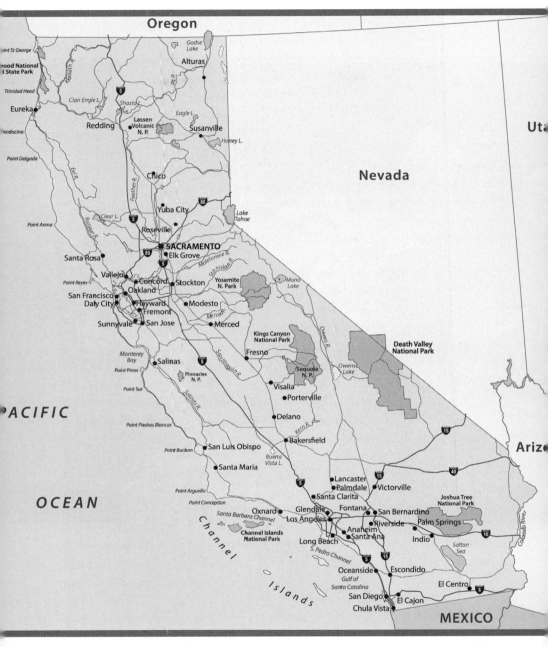

Today, the state of California has many roads, highways, and towns. Some of the most well-known Californian cities share the names of the missions that were built there.

Late chief Charlie Cooke blesses a county supervisor during a dedication ceremony in 2001.

The People and Culture of the Chumash

Development grants have enabled the reservation to provide homes for many families moving to Santa Ynez. New homes continue to be built on the reservation. As of 2016, there were 250 people living on the Santa Ynez Reservation and ninety-seven homes.

As provided in the 1968 Articles of Incorporation, the Chumash at Santa Ynez are represented by their own five-member Business Council. Over the years, the reservation has grown slightly to 127 acres (51 ha). A tribal hall was erected in 1976. A health clinic provides medical care and offers substance abuse programs funded by county and federal agencies. A campground and a thriving casino, both established in 1994, provide employment for tribal members and revenue for reservation programs.

The Chumash have fought for recognition in other ways, too. In May 1978, about twenty-five Chumash people took part in a three-day protest at an ancient burial site in Little Cohu Bay, Point Conception, California. A facility for importing liquefied natural gas was planned for this site. However, an agreement was reached in which the Chumash were allowed to visit the area for religious ceremonies. All ruins and artifacts at the site are protected, and tribal members monitor all excavations.

Santa Ynez Today

Although the Santa Ynez Reservation is still fairly small, revenue from the Chumash Casino Resort has allowed for some economic self-sufficiency. In 2004, the reservation opened a 106-room hotel and a restaurant.

The Chumash Casino Resort has attracted many tourists and locals, and has helped bolster the tribe's economy.

The resort draws about six thousand guests per day, making it a significant contributor to California's tourism industry. The Santa Ynez Reservation also hosts a variety of cultural programming, including an annual tomol crossing. During the tomol crossing, tribe members paddle out to Santa Cruz in a tomol and make their way to where the largest Chumash village was located on the island. Santa Ynez also

The People and Culture of the Chumash

hosts Chumash Culture Days, a two-day event that celebrates the culture of Native Californians with singing, dancing, games, and storytelling. The reservation also houses an environmental office dedicated to maintaining the Chumash values of stewardship in the natural world, a tribal health clinic, and a fire department that protects both the reservation, the citizens of Santa Barbara County, and beyond.

Off-reservation Chumash have formed groups to preserve their heritage as well. One such group is the Wishtoyo Foundation, a nonprofit organization focused on preserving Chumash culture and history. In partnership with the Los Angeles County Department of Beaches & Harbors, the Wishtoyo Foundation created the Wishtoyo Chumash Village, an authentic recreation of an ancient Chumash village. The Wishtoyo Chumash Village hosts cultural workshops in basketry, tomol construction, and language preservation. Tours of the village are also available and it serves to function as a living museum. The village spans 4 acres (1.6 ha) of Nicholas Canyon County Beach in Malibu. The site is known to be a historic home of Chumash ancestors who were believed to occupy the area as early as 4,000 BCE.

While the stories of indigenous people are often focused on degradation and loss, the Chumash

Mati Waiya, ceremonial and executive director of the Wishtoyo Foundation, blesses the Upper Las Virgenes Canyon Open Space Preserve in 2004.

The People and Culture of the Chumash

people are building their own narrative through economic self-sufficiency and cultural preservation. Their numbers may have dwindled from their most prosperous times, but Chumash enthusiasm for their values, culture, and heritage has not. They continue to instill pride in their descendants, and the tribe is working to ensure their culture will be taught, valued, and engaged for generations to come.

Chumash member
Fernando "Kitsepawit"
Librado (*center*) poses
with other Native
members, circa 1912.

CHAPTER SEVEN

Our elders, and the ones before them, have endured so much for us to stay together as a tribe.

—Nakia Zavalla, cultural director for the Santa Ynez Band of Indians

FACES OF THE CHUMASH

Throughout their history, the Chumash have learned about their culture, history, and beliefs through their elders and ancestors, those men and women who kept their culture alive even under extraordinarily trying circumstances. Here are just a few Chumash individuals who resisted the horrors of colonialism and embraced their rightful heritage.

Juan Justo

Juan de Jesús Justo (1858–1941), storyteller and ethnohistorian, was born in the Santa Barbara area ten years after the United States acquired California from Mexico. Juan's father was known as Old Justo. At the time, the Chumash had already suffered greatly—first from the Spanish and Mexicans and then from the

Americans who seized ancestral lands and forced the Chumash to abandon their way of life. Yet Juan's father refused to abandon the traditional practices and beliefs of his people. Old Justo worked with scholars such as Oscar Loew and Henry Henshaw to preserve Chumash vocabulary and identify place names. As Juan grew up, his father and his mother Cecilia made certain that he learned about his heritage.

Juan became well known as a storyteller and an expert on Chumash culture, having a lively and colorful personality. Working with ethnohistorian John P. Harrington and anthropologist Alfred Kroeber, he became central in preserving Chumash history and culture in published documents, sound recordings, photographs, and motion pictures. He was also considered an authority on the Mexican influence on the Chumash people. In 1914, he served as an actor in a film produced by Harrington and Kroeber. Juan provided many of the Chumash stories that Harrington collected in December's Child, a book that has made a major contribution in understanding and preserving Chumash culture. In the late 1930s, Juan worked with Harrington's nephew to make sound recordings of Chumash language in the years before his death in 1941.

Kitsepawit (Fernando Librado) (1839–1915) was born in the seaport of Swaxil on Santa Cruz Island. His paternal grandfather was the leader of the village. His father, grandfather, and great-grandfather were all named Kitsepawit, and each of them resisted both the Spanish and the Mexicans. The Island Chumash were devastated by plagues and attacks by Aleuts working for the Russians in the otter trade. The remaining villagers—mostly women and children—fled to San Buenaventura Mission on the mainland. Here, Kitsepawit was raised by his mother, who taught him the language of the island. When forced to adopt a Mexican name, he chose Librado from the Spanish *libertador,* which means "liberator."

Kitsepawit always identified with his Chumash ancestry and devoted his life to learning about his heritage, even though he had to live under the mission system. By 1845, the Natives living at the missions were left destitute. The California gold rush then brought waves of settlers into the region. Kitsepawit lived in poverty in the Mexican community in Ventura but finally moved to the mountains to work as a sheepherder and ranch hand. During this time, he frequently visited Chumash families and gained valuable knowledge about the traditional lands, village sites, and sacred places of his people.

In his later years, Kitsepawit became friends with John P. Harrington, an anthropologist working with the Smithsonian Institution. Before he died in 1915, Kitsepawit provided Harrington with a wealth of knowledge about Chumash language, culture, and history that would otherwise have been lost. The information he shared is invaluable and includes songs, dances, ceremonies, language, and much more. Harrington took over three hundred thousand pages of notes on Fernando's testimony alone, over three thousand of which detailed canoe building.

The People and Culture of the Chumash

Pacomio (active 1820s) was brought up and educated by the padres at La Purísima Mission, which was located between Santa Barbara and San Luis Obispo. He became a highly skilled carpenter but hated Spanish domination. Angry about the mistreatment of his people, he organized a revolt to drive the Spanish from California. He traveled to other missions to encourage the Native people living there to support the uprising. He also convinced neighboring tribes, such as the Yokuts, to move close to the missions to facilitate a surprise attack.

On the day of the uprising, Pacomio sent messengers to inform his allies. Some messengers reached the missions at Santa Barbara and Santa Inés. However, those going to the northern missions were caught. On March 19, 1824, believed to be the day planned for the attack, Pacomio declared himself to be chief of all the Native peoples of California. He led a force of about two thousand men against La Purísima, captured the mission, and jailed the soldiers. The Native people at Santa Barbara and Santa Inés also revolted. However, other neophytes did not join the uprising, and the Spanish soon counterattacked. The rebellion gradually ended, and Pacomio surrendered. He was allowed to live peacefully at Monterey, but little else is known about this brave man.

Maria Solares (circa 1842–1922), was born near the Santa Inés Mission and lived in that area for her entire life. She was educated in both the traditional Chumash way of life and the Catholic mission system. Her father, Benvenuto Qililkutayiwit, and her paternal grandparents were both from the village of Kalawasaq, located close to the mission. However, by the 1880s, the village had been abandoned as priests moved the inhabitants into housing near the mission. Maria married Manuel Solares, whose father, Raphael Solares, was the last person to serve as a Chumash religious leader.

Maria's mother, Brigada, who was half-Chumash and half-Yokut, was born in the Yokut village of Tinlew just south of present-day Bakersfield, California. When Brigada was dying in 1868, she asked Maria to visit her Yokut and Chumash relatives. Years later, Maria worked with John P. Harrington to record a personal account of her visit. These narratives recounted the experiences of her uncle, Juan Moynal, who served as mayor of Tinlew, and her traditionalist uncle, Sapakay, who never lived among Christian peoples. Maria is regarded as one of John P. Harrington's most important sources of information about the Chumash.

Rafael Solares (1822–1890) was Maria's father-in-law. In the late 1800s, he served as chief of the Santa Ynez Band of Chumash. In 1877, he allowed the French scientist Leon de Cessac, who excavated several Chumash sites, to photograph him in traditional clothing and body decoration. These photographs are some of the oldest photographic evidence of Chumash culture.

From the early Natives who laid the foundation of Chumash values to the modern-day Chumash people focused on preservation of tradition, many individuals have contributed to the culture of Chumash society.

The People and Culture of the Chumash

CHRONOLOGY

9000–6000 BCE Early people live in small bands, harvesting shellfish and hunting game. They use stone tools, make baskets, and fashion bead jewelry. The climate is cool and moist, with sprawling pine forests.

6000–3000 BCE Subsistence activities shift to gathering seeds. This time is known as the Milling Stone Period because of the abundance of milling stones used to grind acorns and the small, hard seeds of grasses that are a principal food. Human population increases. Hunters begin to use the *atlatl* to hunt elk, deer, and sea mammals. People speak an early Chumash language in the Santa Barbara region.

3000–800 BCE Fishing with shell hooks and barbed harpoons and hunting sea mammals becomes more important. The tomol is adopted around 2000 BCE. More abundant fishing leads to the growth of large, permanent villages on the coast. Around 1500 BCE, the bow and arrow replaces the atlatl. Warfare increases during a period of drought.

800 BCE –1772 CE Marine fishing using nets remains a major source of Chumash subsistence. Hunting and gathering wild plants, notably acorns and various seeds, supplement the seafood diet. Two-thirds of the Chumash people live near the coast. People use shell beads, produced mostly on the northern Channel Islands, as money. Trade and warfare become important.

1772 San Luis Obispo is the first of the Spanish missions to be built in Chumash territory.

1772–1822 Traditions of hunting, fishing, and gathering are abandoned in favor of cultivation of crops and raising livestock.

1824 Chumash rise up against the mission system at Santa Inés, La Purísima, and Santa Barbara.

1833 The Mexican government transfers the land holdings of the missions from the Catholic Church to Mexican landowners.

1848 Mexico cedes California to the United States, and the remaining Chumash lands are taken by Americans. Gold is discovered in California.

1849 The California gold rush draws thousands of settlers to California.

1850 California becomes a state and more settlers flood into traditional Chumash territory.

1901 The Santa Ynez Reservation, the smallest in California and the only Chumash reservation, is established.

1978 The Chumash agree to end a three-day protest at one of their ancient burial sites.

1994 A bingo casino is established on the Santa Ynez Reservation to provide a source of tribal income.

2002 Santa Ynez Reservation builds new Tribal Health Clinic; 50 percent of patients are non-Native.

2004 Santa Ynez Reservation opens 106-room hotel and restaurant.

2007 Dr. Richard Applegate and the Santa Ynez Education Committee publish *The Samala-English Dictionary: A Guide to the Samala Language of the Ineseño Chumash People.*

2009 The Wishtoyo Foundation begins a basketry preservation program.

2010 The Wishtoyo Foundation opens the Šmuwič Language School at Wishtoyo's Chumash Village.

2012 Santa Ynez Reservation opens an education center.

2013 The Quicksilver Foundation unveils clothing items inspired by Chumash art. A percentage of proceeds are donated to the Wishtoyo Chumash Village.

2015 Ninth Annual Santa Ynez Chumash Culture Days celebrates Chumash life through singing, dancing, and gaming.

GLOSSARY

adept Skilled in a specific area.

adobe Bricks and building material made of sun-dried mud and straw; also the name of buildings made with this material.

aesthetics A set of principles related to the appreciation of beauty.

'antap A Chumash religious society.

'ap A Chumash dwelling made of poles covered with tule and cattails.

assimilate Integrate into a larger society or culture.

channel A narrow body of water separating two land masses.

chaparral A dense, impenetrable thicket of stiff or thorny shrubs or dwarf trees.

colonialism The practice of imposing political control over an area through occupation and economic exploitation.

enigmatic Mysterious, difficult to interpret.

eradicate To destroy completely.

lexicon The vocabulary of a language.

linguist A person who specializes in the study of languages.

The People and Culture of the Chumash

mission A religious community centered around a church.

missionary A person who preaches a religion, usually the Christian religion, to a group of people often not familiar with the religion.

padre The Spanish name for a priest of the Catholic Church.

paha A ceremonial leader responsible for making speeches and managing dancing and singing at fiestas.

pedagogy The art, science, or profession of teaching.

pictograph A sign or symbol drawn or painted on a rock, cliff, or cave wall.

reverence A feeling or display of honor or respect

shaman A religious leader responsible for the spiritual and physical well-being of the people.

siliyik A dance space used at special times during the year.

solstice The two times in the year (winter and summer) when the sun is farthest north or south of the equator.

temescal The Spanish word for a Chumash sweathouse. Also spelled temascal.

toloache A hallucinogenic drink made from jimsonweed that was taken during religious ceremonies to induce dreams.

tomol A canoe made from wooden planks sewn together.

tule A large bulrush abundant in marshy areas of California.

wot The chief who held the highest position in Chumash society.

BIBLIOGRAPHY

Arnold, Jeanne E. *Foundations of Chumash Complexity.* Los Angeles, CA: Cotsen Institute of Archaeology, University of California, 2004.

Blackburn, Thomas C. *December's Child: A Book of Chumash Oral Narratives.* Berkeley, CA: University of California Press, 1980.

Broyles-González, Yolanda, and Pilulaw Khus. *Earth Wisdom: A California Chumash Woman.* Tucson, AZ: University of Arizona Press, 2011.

Campbell, Paul Douglas. *Survival Skills of Native California.* Salt Lake City, UT: Gibbs Smith, 2000.

Chiles, Frederic Caire. *California's Channel Islands: A History.* Norman, OK: University of Oklahoma Press, 2015.

Gamble, Lynn H. *The Chumash World at European Contact: Power, Trade, and Feasting among Complex Hunter-Gatherers.* Berkeley, CA: University of California Press, 2008.

Haas, Lisbeth. *Saints and Citizens: Indigenous Histories of Colonial Missions and Mexican California.* Oakland, CA: University of California Press, 2013.

Kroeber, A. L. *Handbook of the Indians of California.* New York: Dover Publications, 2012.

Lightfoot, Kent G., and Otis Parrish. *California Indians and Their Environment: An Introduction.* Berkeley, CA: University of California Press, 2009.

Sutton, Mark Q. *An Introduction to Native North America.* 4th ed. Boston, MA: Allyn and Bacon, 2011.

Timbrook, Janice. *Chumash Ethnobotany: Plant Knowledge among the Chumash People of Southern California.* Santa Barbara, CA: Santa Barbara Museum of Natural History, 2007.

FURTHER INFORMATION

Want to know more about the Chumash? Check out these websites, videos, and organizations.

Websites

National Parks Service- Channel Islands

https://www.nps.gov/chis/index.htm

The Channel Islands section of the National Parks Service website allows visitors to learn about the history of the land as well as the past inhabitants. Users can read stories of the Chumash tomol crossing and learn about the lives of Native people.

Our Mother Tongues

http://www.ourmothertongues.org/Home.aspx

Our Mother Tongues is a website that offers a glimpse into a variety of language revitalization movements. Users can learn about endangered indigenous languages.

The People and Culture of the Chumash

Wishtoyo Chumash Foundation

http://www.wishtoyo.org

The Wishtoyo Chumash Foundation website offers an in-depth look at the efforts of the foundation to preserve Chumash culture and history. The site details their education initiatives and environmental stewardship and highlights spiritual wellness.

Videos

Chumash Blessing

https://www.youtube.com/watch?v=SJ5RWXnd99M&feature=youtu.be

Mati Waiya, founder of Wishtoyo Foundation, gives a traditional Chumash blessing in this video.

Chumash History and Culture

https://www.youtube.com/watch?v=ieKc1z9e5as

Georgiana Sanchez, professor of Native American Literature at California State University and Chumash elder, discusses Chumash culture.

Painted Cave

https://www.youtube.com/watch?v=MQzNd_iczRI

In this video, Chumash painted caves are explored and viewers are acquainted with the locations of various Chumash pictographs around Santa Barbara, California.

Organizations

The California Indian Museum and Cultural Center

5250 Aero Drive

Santa Rosa, CA 95403

(707) 579-3004

http://www.cimcc.org

Chumash Indian Museum

3290 Lang Ranch Parkway

Thousand Oaks, CA 91362

(805) 492-8076

http://www.chumashindianmuseum.com/
index.html

Santa Barbara Museum of Natural History

2559 Puesta de Sol Road

Santa Barbara, CA 93105

(805) 682-4711

http://www.sbnature.org

Santa Ynez Reservation

PO Box 517

Santa Ynez, CA 93460

(805) 688-7997

http://www.santaynezchumash.org

INDEX

Page numbers in **boldface** are illustrations. Entries in **boldface** are glossary terms.

games, 32, **32–33**, 34, 75–76, **77**, 103

gathering, 25, 34, 40, 88

gifts, 41, 59, 61, 71, 83–85

good and evil, 20, 66

Harrington, John P., 53, 63, 91, 95, 108–111

health care, 101, 103

housing, **22**, 28–29, **30–31**, 33–34, 111

hunting, 25, 34, 40, 51, 59, 88

hunting rights, 34

Interior Chumash, 11–12, 19, 25, 29

Island Chumash, 11, 42, 55, 57, 92, 109

Justo, Juan de Jesús, 103

Kitsepawit, 51, **106**, 109
Kroeber, Alfred, 108

land ownership, 84, 87, 90–91, 98, 108–109

language, 11, 29, 83, 88, 91–95, 103, 108–110

lexicon, 95

Librado, Fernando, 51, 53, 91, **106**, 109

linguist, 95

marriage, 40–41, 98

men, roles of, 29, 32, 34, 40–43, 47, 51–52, 57, 70, 75–76

messengers, 36, 110

Mexico, 84, 90, 108

Milling Stone people, 13

mission, 62, 84, **86**, 87–91, 98, 109–111

missionary, 11, 86

money, 53–55, **54**, 59, 61

museums, 63, 103

musical instruments, 73

Pacomio, 110

padre, 85, 110

The People and Culture of the Chumash

ABOUT THE AUTHORS

Joel Newsome is a writer living in Florida. He attended Western Michigan University and recently wrote a book about the mythology of elves.

Raymond Bial has published more than eighty books—most of them photography books—during his career. His photo-essays for children include *Corn Belt Harvest, Amish Home, Frontier Home, The Underground Railroad, Portrait of a Farm Family, Cajun Home,* and *Where Lincoln Walked.*

As with his other work, Bial's deep feeling for his subjects is evident in both the text and illustrations. He travels to tribal cultural centers, photographing homes, artifacts, and surroundings and learning firsthand about the national lifeways of these peoples.

The emeritus director of a small college library in the Midwest, he lives with his wife and three children in Urbana, Illinois.